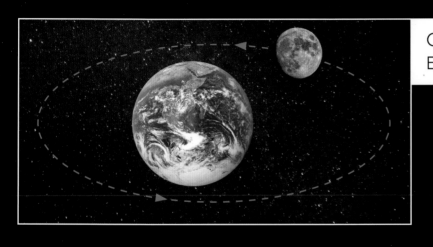

Our
Ear

C000093105

The biggest moon is Ganymede. Ganymede orbits the planet Jupiter in seven days.

Ganymede

our Moon

Saturn

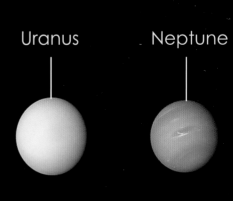

Uranus

Neptune

Saturn's moons
(82 in total)

Uranus's moons
(27 in total)

Neptune's moons
(14 in total)

🔍 LOOK!

Look at the pages.
Which two planets in our Solar System don't have any moons?

What is inside a moon?

Most large moons have three important parts – a core, a mantle and a crust. Inside a moon is a very hard, round core. The mantle of a moon can be **rock** or **ice**. Moons also have a hard crust on the outside.

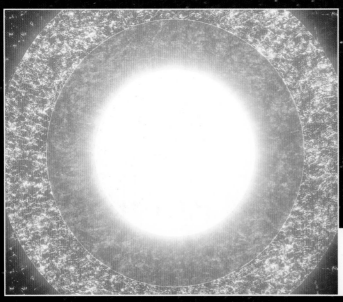

Our Moon's core is very hot.

DO YOU KNOW?

Level 3

MOONS

Written by Adékúnmi Olátúnjí
Series Editor: Nick Coates
Designed by Dynamo Limited

LADYBIRD BOOKS

UK | USA | Canada | Ireland | Australia
India | New Zealand | South Africa

Ladybird Books Ltd is part of the Penguin Random House group of companies
whose addresses can be found at global.penguinrandomhouse.com.
www.penguin.co.uk   www.puffin.co.uk   www.ladybird.co.uk

Penguin
Random House
UK

First published 2023
001

Printed in China

The authorized representative in the EEA is Penguin Random House Ireland,
Morrison Chambers, 32 Nassau Street, Dublin D02 YH68

A CIP catalogue record for this book is available from the British Library

ISBN: 978-0-241-62256-8

All correspondence to:
Ladybird Books
Penguin Random House Children's
One Embassy Gardens, 8 Viaduct Gardens, London SW11 7BW

Contents

New words

astronaut

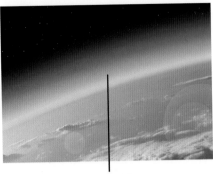

atmosphere

crater

gravity

ice

land
(verb)

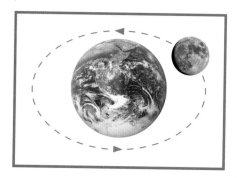

orbit
(verb)

planets

rock
(noun)

scientist

solar system

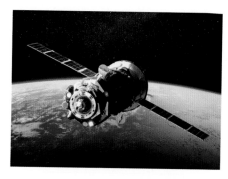

spacecraft

What is a moon?

Our **Solar System** has one sun and eight **planets**. The planets **orbit** the Sun. A moon is smaller and orbits a planet. Some planets have many moons, and some have no moons.

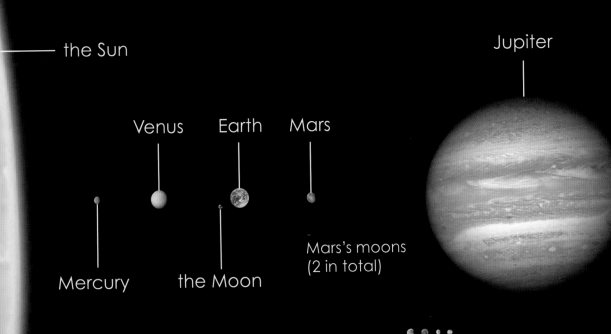

the Sun

Jupiter

Venus   Earth   Mars

Mercury   the Moon

Mars's moons
(2 in total)

Jupiter's moons
(79 in total)

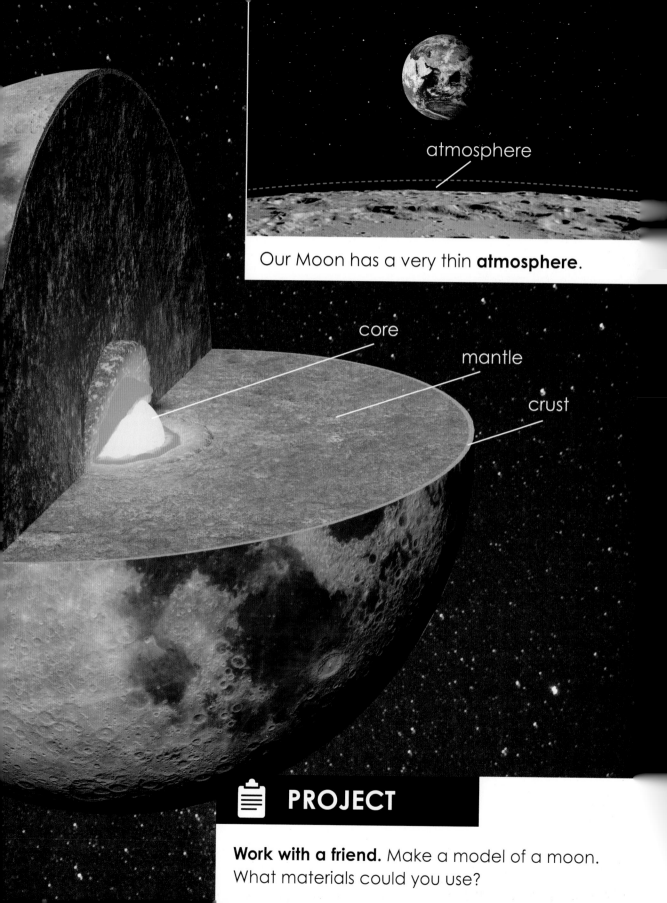

atmosphere

Our Moon has a very thin **atmosphere**.

core

mantle

crust

📋 PROJECT

Work with a friend. Make a model of a moon.
What materials could you use?

Where did our Moon come from?

In the past, the planet Theia hit Earth.

Theia

Parts of Theia and Earth then came together. They made the Moon.

Earth's **gravity** makes the Moon orbit Earth. Gravity on Earth is stronger than on the Moon.

the Moon —

—— Earth

high tide

low tide

The Moon's gravity makes the seas on Earth move up and down.

▶ WATCH!

Watch the video (see page 32).
How old is the Moon?

What can you see on the Moon?

sea

Asteroids can hit planets and moons and make **craters**. Our Moon has many craters because its atmosphere is thin. It can't stop asteroids. When you look at the Moon, you can see the big craters.

You can also see seas on our Moon, but they do not have water. The seas are old rock.

asteroid

Earth has a few craters. Earth's atmosphere stops most asteroids from hitting its crust.

crater

📋 PROJECT

Work with a friend. At the beginning of the month, look up at the Moon. Draw the shape of the Moon and fill in what you see. Repeat every day for one month. How does the Moon change?

How close is the Moon?

The Moon looks close to Earth, but it is not! The Moon is about 384,400 kilometres away from Earth. It looks close because we can see it very well at night.

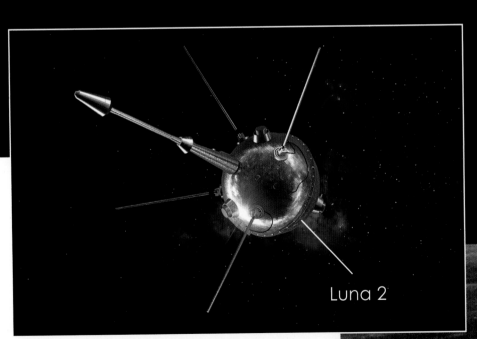

Luna 2

The first **spacecraft** went to the Moon in 1959. There were no people inside. It travelled for more than a day.

Apollo 11

The first **astronauts landed** on the Moon in 1969. They travelled for three days.

📖 **FIND OUT!**

Use books or the internet to find out which country sent the first spacecraft to the Moon.

Can we live on the Moon?

We need water to live, but there is no water on the Moon. There is only ice. The nights are very cold on the Moon because there is little atmosphere. The days are also very hot. We can't live on the Moon now.

One day, **scientists** want to make a place on the Moon for astronauts to live in.

Astronauts must wear spacesuits on the Moon.

old spacesuit

new spacesuit

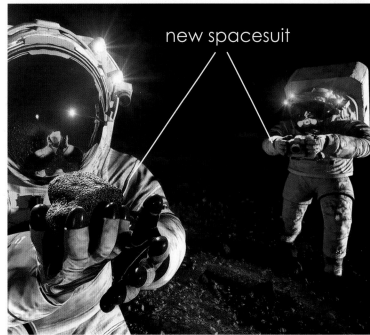

THINK!

Would you like to live on the Moon? Why / Why not?

What is moon dust?

Astronauts came back to Earth with moon dust. Moon dust is little parts of rock from the Moon. Scientists study moon dust to learn about the Moon's past.

Scientists also study other planets and moons. They look for water and study their atmospheres.

Moon dust can tell us a lot about the Solar System.

moon dust

🔍 **LOOK!**

Look at the pages.
What colour is this moon dust?

Can we visit other moons?

Other moons are not as close to Earth as our Moon. Sending people to other moons is difficult and expensive. We send spacecraft to take pictures and then scientists study the pictures.

Europa

Jupiter

Callisto

Ganymede

Io

In 1610, Galileo Galilei was the first person to see moons orbiting Jupiter. The four moons he saw were Ganymede, Europa, Io and Callisto.

Galileo Galilei

Huygens spacecraft on Saturn's moon Titan.

▶ WATCH!

Watch the video (see page 32).

What did Galileo Galilei use to see Jupiter's moons?

What is an icy moon?

There is ice on Earth.
There is some ice on the Moon.
Other moons in our Solar
System have a lot of ice.
These are icy moons.

Enceladus is one of
Saturn's icy moons.

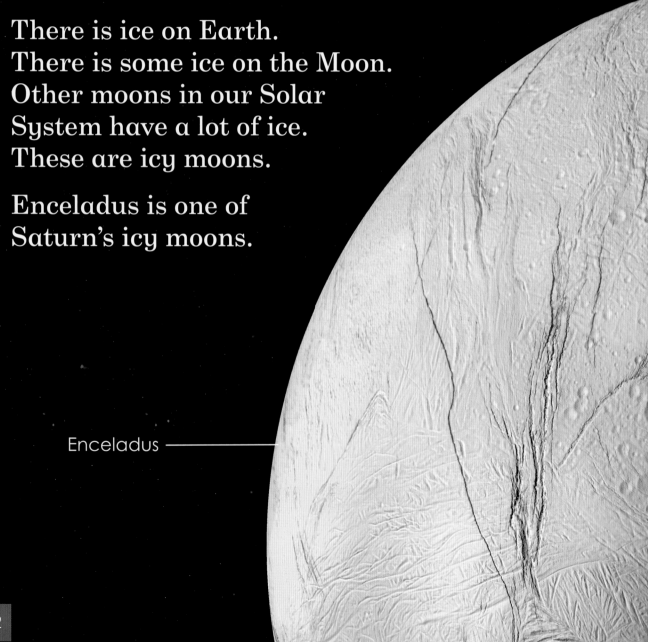

Enceladus

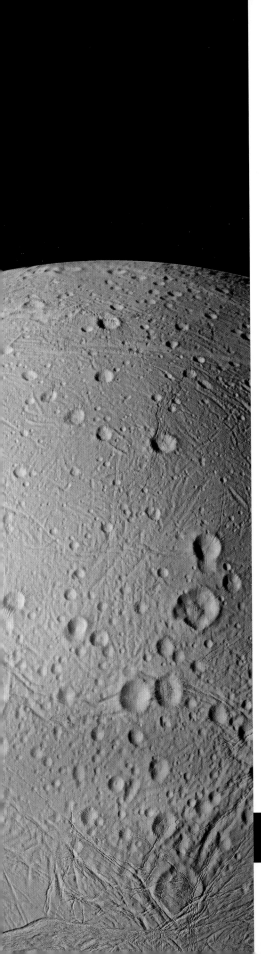

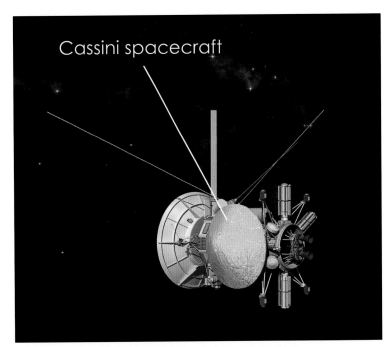

Cassini spacecraft

In 2014, the Cassini spacecraft found water on Enceladus.

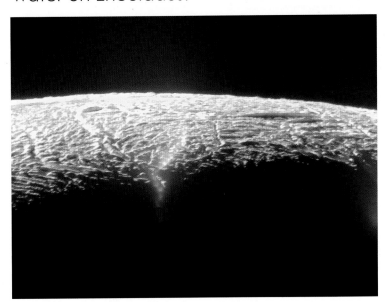

Scientists are looking for things that live on other planets and moons. Maybe they can find them in the water on the icy moons.

 **THINK!**

Why do scientists think that they may find life on moons with water?

Can anything live on other moons?

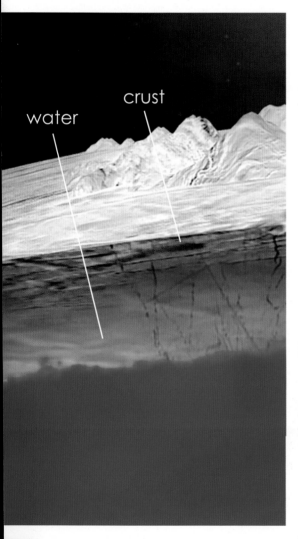

water

crust

Europa

Europa is one of Jupiter's moons. Scientists think that there is more water on Europa than there is on Earth.

Europa's crust is not rock – it is ice. Scientists think that all of Europa's water is below the crust.

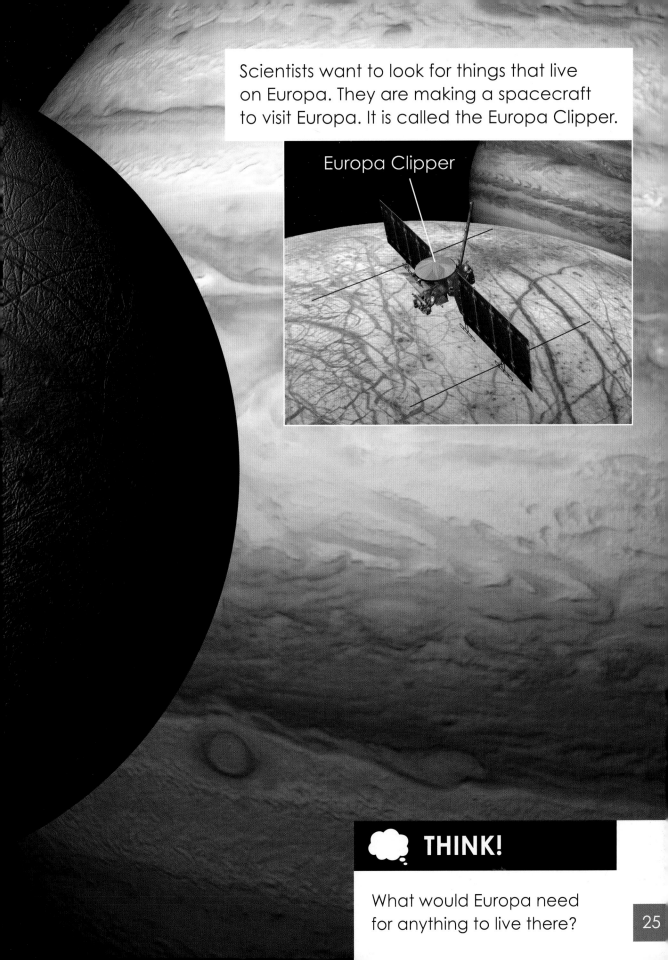

Scientists want to look for things that live on Europa. They are making a spacecraft to visit Europa. It is called the Europa Clipper.

Europa Clipper

THINK!

What would Europa need for anything to live there?

Scientists are also looking for things that live on Titan. Titan is Saturn's largest moon. It is the only moon in our Solar System that has clouds and a thick atmosphere.

Titan ——————

lake

In 2005, the Cassini-Huygens spacecraft took pictures of Titan. The pictures showed rivers, lakes and seas. But there is no water in them. Scientists think that there is water below Titan's ice crust.

Christiaan Huygens was the
first man to see Titan, in 1655.

📖 FIND OUT!

Use books or the internet to find out what the 26
rivers, lakes and seas on Titan's crust are made of.

Can moons have volcanoes?

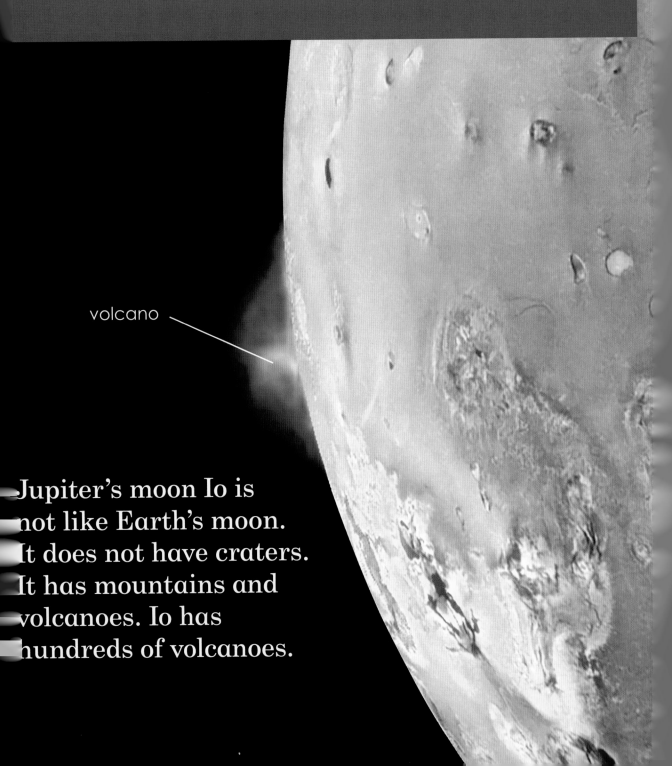

volcano

Jupiter's moon Io is not like Earth's moon. It does not have craters. It has mountains and volcanoes. Io has hundreds of volcanoes.

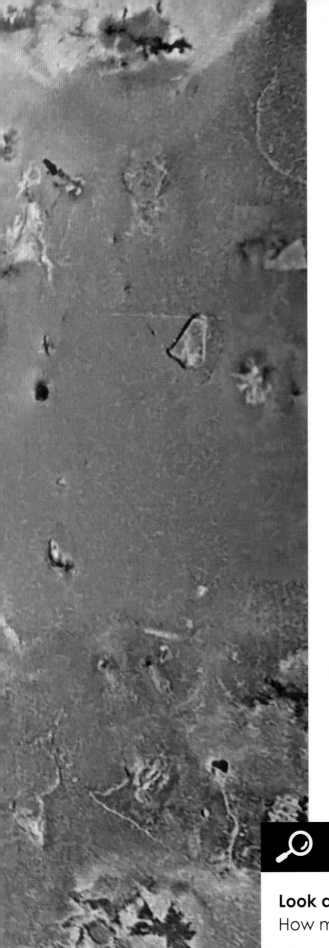

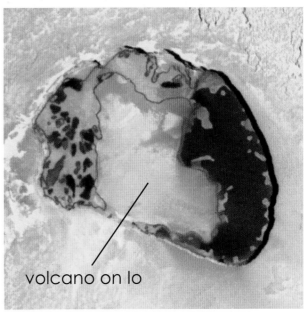

volcano on Io

Most volcanoes on Earth and Io are hot, but some volcanoes in our Solar System are cold. They are ice volcanoes, and they are called cryovolcanoes.

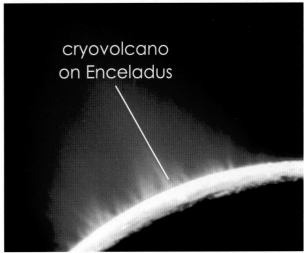

cryovolcano on Enceladus

Cryovolcanoes send ice and snow up and out of the moon's crust.

🔍 LOOK!

Look at the pages.
How many colours can you see on Io?

Quiz

Choose the correct answers.

1 What do moons orbit?
- **a** Theia
- **b** planets
- **c** moons

2 What is the biggest moon in our Solar System?
- **a** Ganymede
- **b** Titan
- **c** Europa

3 What makes craters on the Moon?
- **a** water
- **b** asteroids
- **c** gravity

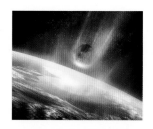

4 What is moon dust?
- **a** water
- **b** ice
- **c** rock

5 Europa is one of the moons of which planet?

   a Earth

   b Saturn

   c Jupiter

6 Who saw the four moons of Jupiter in 1610?

   a Galileo Galilei

   b Neil Armstrong

   c Buzz Aldrin

7 When did Christiaan Huygens first see Titan?

   a 2005

   b 1955

   c 1655

8 Cryovolcanoes are . . .

   a cold volcanoes.

   b hot volcanoes.

   c craters.

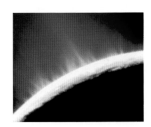

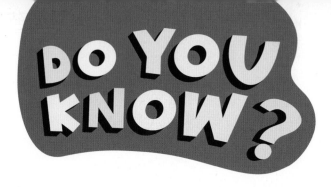

DO YOU KNOW?

Visit www.ladybirdeducation.co.uk for FREE DO YOU KNOW? teaching resources.

- video clips with simplified voiceover and subtitles
- video and comprehension activities
- class projects and lesson plans
- audio recording of every book
- digital version of every book
- full answer keys

To access video clips, audio tracks and digital books:

1 Go to **www.ladybirdeducation.co.uk**
2 Click 'Unlock book'
3 Enter the code below

h8aTjZ0QjQ

Stay safe online! Some of the DO YOU KNOW? activities ask children to do extra research online. Remember:

- ensure an adult is supervising;
- use established search engines such as Google or Kiddle;
- children should never share personal details, such as name, home or school address, telephone number or photos.